Phoebe Waller-Bridge

FLEABAG

NICK HERN BOOKS
London
www.nickhernbooks.co.uk

A Nick Hern Book

Fleabag first published in Great Britain as a paperback original in 2013 by
Nick Hern Books Limited, The Glasshouse, 49a Goldhawk Road, London
W12 8QP, in association with DryWrite and Soho Theatre

Reprinted with revisions in 2014, 2017
Reprinted with a new cover in 2016

Cover image: All3Media and Amazon Studios

Designed and typeset by Nick Hern Books, London
Printed and bound in Great Britain by CPI Books (UK) Ltd

A CIP catalogue record for this book is available from the British Library

ISBN   978 1 84842 624 5

Introduction
Phoebe Waller-Bridge

I am obsessed with audiences. How to win them, why some things alienate them, how to draw them in and surprise them, what divides them. It's a theatrical sport for me – and I'm hooked.

When Vicky Jones (director of the stage play/inimitable genius/excellent friend) and I were producing nights of short plays under our theatre company, DryWrite, we were forever scrabbling for new ways to put the audience in the centre of the experience.

Each experiment illuminated little tricks of how to construct a satisfying story. We would give briefs to writers, challenging them to elicit a specific response from the audience. It would change each time, but one, for example, was: 'Make an audience fall in love with a character in under five minutes.' Writers would write the monologues, actors would perform them, and each audience member would express their 'love' by releasing a small, heart-shaped, helium balloon at the moment they fell in love with the character on stage.

Each writer could measure their success by how many balloons floated to the ceiling of the theatre during their piece. At the end of the night we'd all then charge to the bar and discuss why some pieces succeeded over others. Whatever the experiment, the audience rarely behaved in the way we expected them to, prompting many fascinating conversations and debates about character, story and language that proved invaluable lessons in playwriting.

Over the years, we put on event after event, experiment after experiment, and at the heart of them were always the big questions about how to affect the audience. How do you make people heckle? How do you make people invest in one character over another? How do you make an audience forgive a terrible crime? There was one I was most intrigued by –

'Funny/Not Funny: How do you make an audience laugh in one moment, then feel something completely and profoundly different in the next?'

It was this tightrope that I wanted to walk with *Fleabag*. When we were developing it for the Edinburgh Fringe, I was obsessively looking for ways to surprise the audience, to sneak up on them just when they least expect it.

I knew I wanted to write about a young, sex-obsessed, angry, dry-witted woman, but the main focus of the process was her direct relationship with her audience and how she tries to manipulate and amuse and shock them, moment to moment, until she eventually bares her soul.

Adapting *Fleabag* for TV in 2016 meant this same fundamental structure still applied, but experiments with the audience took another interesting turn and Fleabag's relationship with the audience intensified.

In theatre, people come to you, or your characters. In TV, characters arrive in people's living rooms, their kitchen tables, and are often even taken into bed with them! It's a very intimate way of communicating with an audience and a privilege to experiment with. With this in mind, I was determined for the audience of the TV series to feel like they were having a personal relationship with Fleabag – hence the audience address – and the absolute ideal situation was that at the beginning you should feel she wants you there and by the end, that she wishes she hadn't let you in. A feeling I imagine lots of people have felt after spilling it all out to a stranger.

If there is one thing I've learned, it's that you get a lot for free from an audience if you make them laugh. The power of comedy is astonishing to me – how it can disarm an audience and leave them wide open and vulnerable. Ultimately, for the *Fleabag* audience, I wanted the drama of this woman's story to leap into their open, laughing mouths and find its way deep into their hearts.

This piece was originally written for the BBC Daily Drop in 2016.

Fleabag was first performed at Underbelly on 1 August 2013 as part of the Edinburgh Festival Fringe. It transferred to Soho Theatre, London, on 3 September 2013 and was revived there in May 2014 and December 2016. The cast was as follows:

FLEABAG — Phoebe Waller-Bridge

VOICE-OVERS
FEMALE VOICE (RECEPTIONIST) — Holly Pigott
MALE VOICE — Adam Brace
FEMALE VOICE (LECTURE-HALL TANNOY) — Charlotte McBrearty
LECTURER — Teresa Waller-Bridge
BOO (VOICEMAIL) — Vicky Jones
EX-BOYFRIEND (TEXT MESSAGE) — Charlie Walker-Wise

Director and Dramaturg — Vicky Jones
Producer — Francesca Moody
Designer — Holly Pigott
Associate Designer — Antonia Campbell-Evans
Lighting Designer — Elliot Griggs
Sound Designer — Isobel Waller-Bridge
Associate Sound Designer — Max Pappenheim
Stage Manager — Charlotte McBrearty
PR — Chloé Nelkin Consulting

To Vicky Jones

Note on Text

Other characters can be recorded voices, played by other actors or played by Fleabag.

Pauses and beats are indicated by the space given between lines.

Lights come up on FLEABAG.

She is out of breath and sweating.

FEMALE VOICE. He's ready to see you now.

FLEABAG. Thank you.

    FLEABAG *attempts to hide that she is overheating.*

MALE VOICE. Thanks for coming in today. Really appreciate
    you sending in your CV.

FLEABAG. No problem.

MALE VOICE. It was funny!

FLEABAG. Oh? Okay. That wasn't my intention, but –

MALE VOICE. Great. Our current situation is unusual in that…
    we don't have many… any women working here. Mainly
    due to the –

FLEABAG. Sexual-harassment case.

MALE VOICE. Sexual-harassment case, yes. Are you alright?

FLEABAG. Yes, sorry – I ran from the station. Just a bit hot.
    Sorry. I'm really excited about –

MALE VOICE. Water?

FLEABAG. No, I'm – I'll be okay – actually, yes please, that
    would be great.

    Over the next speech, FLEABAG *pulls her jumper halfway
    over her head exposing her bra. She realises she doesn't
    have a top on underneath and she attempts to pull her
    jumper back down as if nothing had happened.*

MALE VOICE. So we are looking for someone who can handle
    themselves in a competitive environment. It will mainly be
    filing, but we have some pretty good filers so – Haha – yeah.
    It also involves updating the website and throwing up an

occasional twit. It says here that you have done something similar before at the… café that you used to –

Ah okay. Um.

I'm sorry. That won't get you very far here any more.

FLEABAG. Oh no – sorry – I thought I had a top on underneath.

MALE VOICE. Yup. Okay. But for the record.

FLEABAG. No seriously. In this case – genuine accident.

MALE VOICE. Look. With our history here I understand why you might have thought –

FLEABAG. I wasn't trying to – Jesus – I was hot –

MALE VOICE. I take this kind of thing very seriously now.

FLEABAG. I'm not trying to shag you! Look at yourself.

MALE VOICE. Okay. Please leave.

FLEABAG. What!? But I – you don't understand. I need –

MALE VOICE. Please just leave.

 FLEABAG *starts to leave. She turns back.*

FLEABAG. Perv.

MALE VOICE. Slut.

FLEABAG. Wow.

MALE VOICE. Please leave.

FLEABAG. You please leave.

MALE VOICE. It's my office.

FLEABAG. Yeah?

MALE VOICE. Okay.

 Sound effect of feet walking away and a door opening.

FLEABAG. Wait.

Footsteps stop.

–

FLEABAG *turns to the audience.*

Three nights ago I ordered myself a very slutty pizza.

I mean, the bitch was dripping.

That dirty little stuffed-crust wanted to be in me so bad, I just ate the little tart like she meant nothing to me, and she loved it.

That pretty much nailed that, and it was pretty late by now, so I dragged myself upstairs and got into my office – or… my bed – and tried to work on the figures for the café. I run a guinea-pig-themed café. But it's out of cash and it's going to close unless a cheque falls out of the sky, or a banker comes on my arse, but neither are going to happen, and I don't want to dignify the banker-man with a proper mention so I'm not going to talk about him or how I do sometimes wish I could own up to not having morals and just let him come on my arse for ten thousand pounds, but apparently we're 'not supposed to do that', so okay. I *won't*. Even though it would solve *everything*. I won't.

Even though I could.

Lying in my office, the café numbers start to jump out at me like little ninjas, so I rationalise it would be good to just switch off for a bit. Improve my mind. So I watched a pretty good movie, actually, called *17 Again* with Zac Efron who is… fit.

I know.

But seriously, he's actually a – a really good actor. So – Yeah, but the film could have been worse – honestly. Check it out.

Then that finished. So I lay there. Thinking. Café. Numbers. Numbers. Zac. Numbers.

Googled Obama to keep up with – y'know. Who, as it turns out, is also – attractive.

Lay there. Numbers, numbers, Obama, numbers, Zac, Obama, numbers, Zac –

Suddenly I was on YouPorn having a *horrible* wank.

Found just the right sort of gangbang.

Now that really knocked me out, so I put my computer away, leaned over, kissed my boyfriend Harry goodnight and went to sleep.

–

I wake in the morning to find a note from Harry, which reads

'That was the last straw.'

Which is… pretty out of the blue if I'm honest. Didn't know he was counting straws. But nice to know he was paying attention. All his stuff was gone. And everything in the fridge. I was a bit thrilled by his selfishness. Suddenly fancied him again. But relieved one of us did something – he used to say things to me like

HARRY. You're not like other girls… you can… keep up.

FLEABAG (*ponderous*). Keep up.

I stood staring at a handprint on my wall from when I had a threesome on my period. Harry and I break up every twelve to eighteen months and when we do, well…

I wish I could tell you my threesome story was sticky and awkward and everyone went home a little bit sad and empty, but… it was lovely.

Sorry.

I admire how much Harry commits to our break-ups. The fridge is a new detail, but he does always go the extra mile. A few times he's even cleaned the whole flat. Like it's a crime scene. I've often considered timing a break-up around whenever the flat needs a bit of a going-over, but I never know what's going to set him off. Keeps me on my toes.

I sit on the loo and think about all the people I can have sex with now.

I'm not obsessed with sex.

I just can't stop thinking about it.

The performance of it. The awkwardness of it. The drama of it. The moment you realise someone wants your body… not so much the feeling of it.

I've probably got about a week before Harry comes back. I should get on it.

Okay.

Into the shower. Boom. Bedroom. Make-up. Boom. Gonna really make an effort. I take half an hour trying to look nice and I end up looking… *amazing*. I mean, best in ages. One of those days. Boom.

Gorgeous, fresh-faced, heels, wearing a *skirt*, new top, little bit sexy, on my way to *save my* café and yes, I am strutting.

I see a man walking towards me from the bus stop. He can't take his eyes off me. I'm all walking like I've got a paintbrush up my arse, thinking:

Yeah, check me out, cos it's never gonna happen, Chub Chub.

–

I opened the café with my friend Boo. She's dead now. She accidentally killed herself. It wasn't her intention, but it wasn't a total accident. She didn't think she'd actually die, she just found out that her boyfriend slept with someone else and wanted to punish him by ending up in hospital and not letting him visit her for a bit. She decided to walk into a busy cycle lane, wanting to get tangled in a bike. Break a finger, maybe. But it turns out bikes can go fast and flip you into the road. Three people died. She was such a dick. I didn't tell her parents the truth. I told her boyfriend. He cried. A lot.

–

Chub Chub's getting closer. Oversized jacket. Meaty face. Looks me up and down. It's like he's confused about how attractive I am – he can't quite believe it. I worry for a second I'm going to make a sex offender out of the poor guy. He's about to say something. Here we fucking go, this better be good. He's passing, he's passing. He clears his throat, brings his hand to his mouth and coughs:

CHUB CHUB. Walk of shame.

FLEABAG. It's too late to go home and change. I have some flat shoes in my bag and anyway, he's fat.

And he can't take that off at night.

–

Harry's a bit fat. He lightly pats his belly, like he's a little bear. Proud of what he's achieved. Hunted. Gathered. Eaten. Pat. Evidence. Pat, pat. It makes me laugh. A pretty girl at a party once asked me if I secretly liked that Harry had a little paunch, because it made him less attractive to other women. Her boyfriend was the whale in the corner, blocking the door to the toilets.

I asked her if he made her wash the bits he can't reach. She slapped me. Actual slap.

Which means he did.

–

Boo's death hit the papers.

'Local café girl is hit by a bike and a car and another bike.'

There was a buzz around the café all of a sudden. Flowers, notes, guinea-pig memorabilia were left outside in her memory.

Boo made sense of the guinea-pig theme. She was all small and cute and put pictures of guinea pigs everywhere. I pretend they're not there. Which I suspect makes the whole guinea-pig-café experience a bit creepy.

Boo was built a bit like a guinea pig. No waist or hips. Straight down. She rocked it. And she was *beautiful*. Tricky though. Jealous. Sensitive. But beautiful and… my best friend.

–

Ten past eleven at the café. Quiet. Eerily so. Boo always used to play music, read out horoscopes and shrivel crisp packets in the microwave. Used to make the place stink, but she'd turn the little packets into key rings and give them to the people who were especially polite.

One guy in the corner drinking tap water and using the plug. He should buy something, but it's just nice to have someone around. He's reading. He's quite attractive actually, but he doesn't look at me. Even when I purposefully drop a cucumber so I have something to bend over for.

Even Joe hasn't turned up.

Joe's always here at eleven. Proper old geezer, cockney from the toes up, one of life's good people. Huge teeth, white hair, ludicrous grin and a joy that slaps you in the face until you can't help but smile at it. Even the fucking furniture loves Joe. I swear the door swings open voluntarily when he arrives, if only to give the man an entrance. Suddenly he'll just be there. *CRASH*. It almost clatters off its hinges with the force of him.

Nothing touches Joe. He's invincible. You can hear him bellowing 'ALLO, SWEETPEA' to the whole street before he swaggers in, long white hair blowing behind him, cut-off checkered trousers and white T-shirt with braces, dripping wet from the rain all:

JOE. Alright, magic. What a beautiful morning! I can't get over how glorious it is out there. Lucky to live, eh. Lucky to live.

FLEABAG. I don't know what he does. I just know he comes in at eleven.

Usually.

Find myself watching the door. Didn't notice he was such a regular when Boo was here, but now…

But then it's okay, because I see his silhouette take up the window and wait for the door to crash open. But today it just flops to its side with a whimper and Joe limply shuffles to the counter.

I'm not prepared for this.

Alright, Joe?

JOE. Yeah… yeah. I'm alright, ducky.

FLEABAG. Tea, Joe?

JOE. Yeah lovely, lovely. Thank you, darlin'. I'm just gonna… be out the back.

FLEABAG. I make his tea. Six sugars. I take it outside and place it on his little table. He rolls a fag and watches the cup steam.

JOE. Now, ain't that a beautiful thing.

FLEABAG. Not sure what to… I ask him for a rollie. I don't smoke. Well I do, but – shut up.

Can I have a rollie, Joe?

JOE. Sugarplum, you can have anything you want. May I have the honour?

FLEABAG. Yeah, thanks.

He rolls it with his spindly, inky fingers. Takes four seconds. Proper pro. I take it and light it. We smoke. I sit beside him. Two of us on tiny little kids' chairs – sort of a gimmick thing, but really they were cheaper. He looks ridiculous.

JOE. I *love* these chairs y'know.

FLEABAG. What's… wrong, Joe?

JOE (*sighs*). Ah my girl, I just… I love people. I *love* people. But… they get me down.

FLEABAG. Yeah. People are… shit.

He turns and I can see into every deep line on his face.

JOE. Oh no, darlin'. People are *amazing*, but… when will people realise… that people are all we got?

FLEABAG. He smiles, but I feel a bit ambushed. I pretend I have to wash the cappuccino machine, go inside and wipe the nozzle a bit.

–

Five o'clock. Northern line. I'm trying to read an article about how the word 'feminist' has apparently become dirty. I try to engage, but it just makes me think of a bunch of dirty little feminists. I snort-laugh at myself, and then catch the eye of an Attractive Looking Man. Oooh. Well, he is attractive when holding his paper up to here – it all gets a little rodenty from the nose down, but good enough for some eye-fucking on the Tube. He smiles at me with his tiny mouth. I smile back.

He looks down. I look down.

Then we both look up at the same time!

Little giggle. Other people in the carriage start to notice, *charmed* by the moment.

It's revolting.

The Tube is pulling in to Tottenham Court Road.

We both stand up at the same time.

I could vomit.

He says

TUBE RODENT. This doesn't happen very often, does it?

FLEABAG. I give a horribly giggly 'No! No, I suppose it's… quite… rare… yeah…'

He says this may sound crazy, but he has this crazy idea and the crazy idea is to take my number.

We give credit to the moment and exchange numbers.

–

I come out of the Tube and have a Harry panic. He just –
won't be there any more. Madam Ovary is telling me to
RUN BACK TO SAFE PLACE. YOU CAN MAKE BABY
IN SAFE PLACE. But I've got to ride it out. He'll text me
later. The fridge means nothing. Ride it out. I met a nice
rodent on the Tube. I have a lot to be thankful for.

–

FEMALE VOICE. Welcome to Women Speak. The lecture will
commence in five minutes. Please have your tickets ready.

FLEABAG. I find my sister outside the lecture hall. She is
uptight and beautiful and probably anorexic, but clothes look
awesome on her so…

Mum died two years ago. She had a double mastectomy and
never really recovered. It was particularly hard because she
had amazing boobs. She used to say I was lucky because
mine will never get in the way. When I asked her what she
meant she used to demonstrate by pretend-struggling to open
the fridge door, or pretending not to be able to see what's on
the floor.

My sister's got whoppers. But she got all of Mum's good bits.

Dad's way of coping with two motherless daughters was to
buy us tickets to feminist lectures, start fucking our
godmother and eventually stop calling.

These lectures are every three months. It's virtually the only
time I see my sister. She looks tired. We sit in the waiting
room. I realise I'm wearing the top that she 'lost' years ago,
so this is going to be tense.

She really fucking loved this top.

Her eyes fix on it. But – and I can see her brain ticking – she
decides to bank it for later. Makes me nervous. Ammo.

She's reading her 'Kindle'.

She's done her hair a bit fancy, I wonder if she's going out
after the lecture or if she's just got her period. She always does

something a bit different around her period. She gets really
bad PMT. Mum called it a Monthly Confidence Crisis, but it's
PMT. The only way she can get through it is to reinvent
herself in some small way. One particularly bad month, she
came into the kitchen on the brink of tears, in full Lycra. Even
Dad had to leave the room. She looked like she'd climbed into
a condom. It was an emotionally complex couple of days,
which we're not allowed to talk about any more.

She's sitting so still. She's definitely having a monthly
confidence crisis. I mean it's in plaits. Both sides. Sort of tied
at the top. It's unbearable. I can't resist.

(*To* SISTER.) Hair looks nice.

SISTER. Fuck off.

FLEABAG (*to audience*). Brilliant.

She asks about work and I get all spiky. I tell her the café's
lease is up in two days unless I can find at least five grand,
which is impossible. So I'm having to deal with letting go of
the only thing I have left of Boo, and the only thing that's
going to save me from becoming a corporate lady-slave like
her, and that I know everyone thought I'd fuck it up, and
now it looks like I've fulfilled everyone's expectations,
which I didn't mean to say, it just falls out, and now I'm
gonna get her smugness all up in my face.

She just looks at me. No reaction.

I know the rules, so I ask her about *her* super-high-powered,
perfect job-work-super-life. She tells me she's finally been
offered the wet-dream of a job in Finland. Apparently they
want to overpay and underwork her and she won't have to
wear power suits any more.

(*To* SISTER.) Wow. Finland!

But she's turning it down, because her husband says she
shouldn't go, because of Jake.

Jake is her stepson. He's really weird, probably clinically, but no one talks about that. He freaks out if she's away longer than a day and he's got this thing about trying to get into the bath with her. He's fifteen.

I tell her

(*To* SISTER.) He's not your son.

SISTER. That's not the point.

FLEABAG *makes a face*.

Don't make that face.

FLEABAG. I didn't make a face. Go! This is about *you*.

SISTER. I knew you'd say that.

FLEABAG. I tell her she's making a mistake, she shouldn't let other people get in the way of what she really wants and Finland is what she really wants.

She tells me her *husband* isn't 'other people'. That her *husband* is her life.

I tell her her *husband* tried to touch me up at Christmas.

I don't know why I said it. It's true, but he was drunk so...

Martin's always drunk. Which is odd because she is so straight. Maybe that's not odd. But he's very good at being drunk, in that he's FUN DRUNK! No one wants to admit there's a problem, because then they don't get to have 'crazy nights' with 'fun drunk Martin' any more.

(*Scottish accent*.) Martin.

He's one of those men who is explosively sexually inappropriate with everyone. But then makes you feel bad if you take offence because he was just being FUN. You can tell him you are 'popping to the loo' and he'll say –

MARTIN. Aye you pop to the loo, then pull your knickers down and I'll come and FUCK you!

FLEABAG. Claire always tries to sort of half-laugh like she gets the joke, which isn't even a joke.

FEMALE VOICE. Welcome to Women Speak. Sorry for the delay. The lecture will begin shortly. There is no food or drink permitted in the auditorium.

FLEABAG. She just stares at me.

Her neck goes red. I've only see that happen once before.

Then she stares ahead of her.

I give her half my sandwich. Which she eats. Maybe she isn't anorexic… maybe clothes just…

Bitch.

We just sit and wait. Eating the sandwich.

Can't read her. Never been able to read her.

She pulls out a card from Dad and puts it on the seat between us. It's probably still there.

FEMALE VOICE. Women's Speak is about to commence. Please enter the auditorium.

Sound of hubbub.

FLEABAG. The lecture hall is huge. We go right to the front and sit down. Still can't read her.

Suddenly she says

SISTER. I'm going to go to fucking Finland.

FLEABAG. Okay.

SISTER. I hate these suits.

FLEABAG. Okay.

SISTER. How much do you need to save Boo's café?

FLEABAG. About five grand.

SISTER. Okay. I'll transfer it tomorrow. But I don't want to come to these any more.

FLEABAG. Okay.

SISTER. And I want my top back.

FLEABAG. Okay. Thanks, Claire.

Sound of a female lecturer testing the mic. FLEABAG *pays attention.*

LECTURER. Gosh look at you all! Thank you so much for coming. I am overwhelmed by how many faces I see before me. I hope I do your efforts justice with what I have to say this evening. But before I begin, I want to ask you a question. The same question that inspired me to give this lecture. The same question that was posed to women all around this country with, well frankly, shocking results. Now, I don't know about you, but I need some reassurance. (*Little laugh.*) So, I pose the same question to the women in this room today: please raise your hands if you would trade *five years* of your *life* for the so-called 'perfect body'?

FLEABAG *throws her hand in the air.*

FLEABAG. Both of us.

Four hundred women stare at us, horrified.

We are *bad* feminists.

After the lecture Claire says she's going home to talk to Martin.

I want to ask her if she'd have a drink with me before she goes, but I don't know how, so I just watch her plaits disappear into the crowd outside the Tube.

–

Text from Rodent

TUBE RODENT. Still smiling! Smiley face.

FLEABAG. Aw.

I text back: You free now?

He is. We meet up and get very, very drunk. I can't stop
staring at his tiny mouth – he is telling me a story like he
doesn't want to let the words out.

He tells me his sister is deaf, which is his way of letting me
know he is interesting and sensitive. Which is fine. But then
he is the only one in his family who didn't learn sign
language so… Apparently, because they grew up together,
she can lip-read him. Which makes me wonder what she
thinks he is saying all the time, because to me it looks like
Oooo OOOoo Oooo.

He says his sister is so instinctive. She can read people
brilliantly. How she'd be able to read me.

He's having an excellent time.

–

Harry has terrible instincts. Once – I think this may be the best
thing he has ever done – Once, he went to a restaurant – he's
quite shy really – he went to a restaurant having had a filthy
night out with me the night before. I mean, the man was
hanging. He was having lunch with these important website
bods, when it hit him. Halfway through the starter. Yeah. He
was gonna be sick. Like, now. He excused himself, and hurry-
walked to the loo. He burst in – knowing by now that this was
going to be a projectile affair – but all the urinals were taken
and all the cubicles were locked and he couldn't bring himself
to spew in a sink so, in a panic, he kicked down the door of
one of the cubicles revealing a man having a shit. Then boom.
It just aaallll caaaame ooouuut – he puked all over the guy sat
there, all over his shirt, his cock, his legs, his hands, his
boxers, the wall, round his ankles, drenched him.

But then – and this is the best bit – in the frenzy of it all, Harry
rationalised –

HARRY. Oh God, I've just puked on this guy – he is going to
punch me.

FLEABAG. So he smacked him in the face.

Isn't it beautiful? It was particularly good because when he
first told me and Boo he didn't know it was a funny story.
It will never be heard like that again. It was such a serious

story. He was *mortified*. Boo loved poo stories, so couldn't actually deal with the glory of this one. She just stared, mouth open, paralysed with joy as he told it.

–

A few weeks ago, when Harry thought I was sleeping he rolled over, stroked my hair and whispered

HARRY (*whispered*). Where have you gone? Where have you gone?

FLEABAG. He thinks I'm neglecting him, but when your heart is – wish he'd just fuck me. All he wants to do is make love.

He's wasting me. I was once fucking a man who would breathe on every thrust, 'you're so *young,* you're so *young.*'

I masturbate about that all the time. I masturbate a lot these days. Especially when I'm bored or angry or upset or happy.

–

Sound of the Tube.

Last Tube. Attempting to kiss Tube Rodent. It's like target practice with a very small moving target.

I ask him back to mine, but he says he's got work tomorrow.

I say I can come back to his, but he says it's an early start.

I say I'll get him a cab to work in the morning, but he says that's ridiculous.

I say 'what the fuck's your problem' and he says nothing he'd just like to see me again, not rush.

I tell him he's a prick. He says he's 'not sure what's going on'.

I tell him he's a pathetic excuse for a man and leave him at the barriers. Ha.

It's a bit weird then, because we have to come down the same escalator. Push my bum out a bit. Give him some perspective.

I turn around at the platform, but he's gone.

–

At the end of the platform, sat on the bench thing, is the drunkest girl I have *ever* seen. Head rolled forward, tit hanging out, bag sprawled. Nicely dressed, normal-looking girl who had clearly just had one hell of a night. Last Tube rolls in. She doesn't move. I nudge her awake and she stumbles onto the carriage only to slump into a seat, head rolling, other tit folding out now, bag tangled in her feet. I ask her where she is getting off, she says

Slumps back, mouth open. No movement.

DRUNK GIRL. 'Waterloo.'

FLEABAG. Okay, my stop. I help her off, I ask her where she needs to get to next.

DRUNK GIRL. London Bridge…

FLEABAG (*to* DRUNK GIRL). Okay.

DRUNK GIRL. And then Kent.

FLEABAG. Tubes are finished, so we are finding an Overground to London Bridge. At one point, we are walking, and she just falls flat on her face. Boom. Get her up. Keep going. Her head is going all over the place. I'm trying to keep her talking. After about forty-five minutes – *forty-five* – we are on an escalator, and there is a little lull. Then she turns to me and says

DRUNK GIRL. Aw… you're such a lovely man.

–

FLEABAG. Her train pulls in. I don't let go of her.

I ask her if she'd rather come home with me, but she just says

DRUNK GIRL (*grinning*). How dare you… Naughty boy… no!

FLEABAG. So I push her into the carriage and she's gone.

–

I leave the station and think, 'what's one more'. I go into a bar. It is a *business* bar. People are doing *business*. I drink a lot and pretend I am in *business*. A sweaty, bald man cups my vagina from behind at the bar. But he buys me a drink so – he's nice actually. He disappears after a while. Then the business bar closes. (*Slurring slightly.*) Closed for business. Shutting up shop.

That's what Boo said every time we closed the café.

BOO. Shutting up shop!

FLEABAG. Like she was drunk. Which we often were. We'd close up, sink a bottle of wine. Boo would play the ukulele and we'd make up filthy songs. For hours.

(*Singing.*)
    'Another lunch break, another abortion.
    Another piece of cake, another two, fuck-it, twenty
        cigarettes.
    And we're happy, so happy to be modern women.'

–

Suddenly I'm at a familiar doorstep. I ring the bell. And ring the bell. And hammer at the door. And yell like a goat. This should be humiliating. Howling through a man's letter box in the middle of the night, but I'm rolling with it.

A light goes on. I see his silhouette as he trudges down the stairs. He must recognise mine through the door, because his body language changes suddenly. He slowly unhooks the latch and opens the door.

He looks like shit.

I put my hand right over his face and push it a bit. Strikes me as something I'd never thought I'd do to a parent, but it feels right at the time.

He stands in the doorway in his boxer shorts and a T-shirt. I can see the shape of his little manboobs.

(*To* DAD, *very drunk.*) Alright, Dad!

DAD. What's going on?

FLEABAG. I'm absolutely fine.

DAD. Okay.

FLEABAG. I just –

DAD. Yes?

FLEABAG. Nothing.

DAD. Okay?

FLEABAG (*drunkenly*). Okay… I don't… yeah… uh… what? It's a… hm… okay fuck it. Okay.

I have a horrible feeling I'm a greedy, perverted, selfish, apathetic, cynical, depraved, mannish-looking, morally bankrupt woman who can't even call herself a feminist.

He looks at me.

DAD. Well… You get all that from your mother.

FLEABAG (*to* DAD). Good one.

I wonder if he'd find me attractive. If I wasn't his daughter.

(*To* DAD.) If you saw me on the internet. Would you click on me?

DAD. I'm going to call you a cab, darling.

FLEABAG. He lets me wait in his living room while he calls me a cab. I can hear my godmother trying to be quiet at the top of the stairs.

When the cab comes he gently puts me into it and gives me twenty quid.

–

I'm in a *cab*. I can go *anywhere*. So I tell him to take me to… my *flat*.

Already thinking about what I'm going to look up.

–

Back at the flat. I turn on the TV and cry for a bit.

–

I think about a girl called Lily, who I used to touch a bit when we got drunk. Harry didn't know, but girls don't count. I text her. She lives quite close, I think.

Suddenly I'm on PornHub, wet as a beach towel, but I can't get there because the girl has spots on her arse. Some of them just don't make the effort.

–

Nothing back from Lily. I start thinking about this ginger guy I met at a festival last summer.

It was a month after Boo died. I'd taken a pill, and flown off into the woods. I was desperate to get away from Harry. He had started to hug me relentlessly, always telling me how much he loved me, asking how much I loved him, checking if I was 'okay'. There was a rave in the wood. I was panicking and touching my face a lot. Suddenly he was there – ginger guy. He told me to follow him. That he'd take me back to my tent. We were walking for ages. He was holding me by my wrist. At one point he picked me up. It was very dark. I couldn't work out where we were. He wouldn't put me down. He was holding my legs really tightly. Said I was too weak to walk and that I had to trust him. Eventually we stopped. I felt him lie me down in a tent on my back. And then he… he…

He put a cover over me, and a bottle of water by my arm and sat outside until I fell asleep.

Thought he could have at least tried to touch me up a *bit*. Never quite let that go.

–

I text him. Tell him I'm single and horny. He gets back saying he's out, and can be here in twenty minutes. Great. Quickly drink half a bottle of wine, shower, shave everything. Decide I'm going to up my game a bit. Dig out some Agent Provocateur business – suspender belt, the whole bit. Open the door to him. 'Hellooo.' We get to it immediately. After some pretty standard bouncing, I realise he is edging towards my arsehole. I'm drunk, and owe him a 'thank you' for being nice to me at the festival, so... I let him. He's thrilled.

The next morning I wake to find him sitting on the bed, fully dressed, gazing at me. He says that last night was incredible – which I think is an overstatement – but he goes on to say it was particularly special because he has never managed to actually... up-the-bum with anyone before – to be fair, he does have a large penis – and although it was always a fantasy of his, he'd never found anyone he could do it with. He touches my hair and thanks me with genuine earnest. It's sort of moving. He kisses me gently. I kiss him back. Then he leaves.

And I spend the rest of the day wondering...

Do I have a massive arsehole?

–

Five to eleven at the café. I'm still thinking about it.

Haven't heard from my sister. No transfer yet. Wonder if Martin's murdered her, and is now stalking round the city looking for me.

The door smashes open. Joe.

JOE. ALLO, SWEETPEA!

FLEABAG. His legs are too long for his body.

JOE. Look at this beauty!

FLEABAG. He holds up a ukulele that someone just gave him in the pub last night.

Just gave him a ukulele.

He says he's written a song.

I don't want to hear it.

He pulls out another ukulele that apparently another person gave him in another pub.

JOE. Crazy 'ow the world speaks to you all at once eh!

FLEABAG. He says he'll sing his song to me. Then he'll teach it to me. So we can both sing it to Hilary.

I tell him I'm too busy and sit in the back until I hear him leave.

He tinkles a bit, but I don't hear him sing.

–

Schoolkids used to come to the café. Mainly because of Hilary.

Basically, I'm shit at presents and for Boo's birthday two years ago I panicked and bought her a guinea pig. She called it Hilary and now I'm stuck with it.

I don't feel anything about guinea pigs. They're pointless. But Boo took Hilary very seriously as a gift. And then everything became guinea-pig related.

–

I think she was just relieved to have a different animal associated with her. When she was about five, she mentioned, on a childish whim, that she liked owls. For the rest of her life she got owls. Owl duvet covers, owl pens, books about owls, trips to owl sanctuaries. She fucking hated owls. Show her an owl and she'd lose her shit. What she really liked – and I knew this – was screwdrivers. Crazy about them. We'd spend hours unscrewing things, then screwing them back up. She slept with screwdrivers under her pillow until she was about ten.

Come to think of it, a screwdriver would have been a better present than a guinea pig.

–

Midday. Still haven't heard from my sister. Martin's going to
hate me. I picture his massive, Scottish head. Hope he hasn't
beaten the shit out of her or anything. No, he'd never do
something as sexy as that.

I'm joking. Jesus.

–

Hilary is fat and ginger with frizzy bits. Like Annie, the
orphan. If she was grown up. And fat. And a guinea pig.
Which – well, who knows what became of her.

She has this punky bit of fur that explodes off the crown of
her head and falls over her eyes. Makes her look pretty
badass. She has a really straight expression. Boo always said,
if Hilary was in a band, she'd be the guitarist who takes the
music very seriously. She did take music seriously actually.
Whenever Boo played stuff in the café she'd be all –

*Plays some beats. Nods like Hilary. No expression, but
totally in rhythm.*

She's also a sneaky little shit. She knows how to open her
hutch door. I've seen her do it. She pushes the little wood
stopper until it drops out and the door just swings open. She
then freezes, as if she hasn't done anything, then she actually
turns around – and lowers herself down onto the counter,
little legs kicking, looking over her shoulder – checking…
checking… She often does a little poo in the excitement.
Once landed, she creeps along the counter all the way to the
window. Then, when she gets there, in her frenzy of
freedom, she sits down and looks out. Watching the world.

If she wants me to think she's really profound and poetic
doing that, I'm not rising to it.

–

Apparently guinea pigs need other guinea pigs. Or they can
die of loneliness.

But Hilary didn't need a mate. She got more than enough
attention. The punters loved her, she was always on someone's
lap, and she had Boo, who never left her alone. They adored

each other. The morning Boo's boyfriend told her he'd fucked someone else... she walked right past me, took Hilary out of her hutch and sat out the back with her for hours.

I once read a story from the paper to Boo and Hilary about how a little kid repeatedly stuck rubber-ended pencils up the class hamster's arsehole, because he liked it when their eyes popped out. He was sent to a juvenile bootcamp.

I read it out as a bit of a joke, but Boo was *distraught*.

BOO. They sent him away? But he needs help!

FLEABAG. She was a surprising person.

(*To* BOO.) Yeah. He pencil-fucked a hamster.

BOO. He's obviously not happy. Happy people don't do things like that.

FLEABAG. Fair point.

BOO. And anyway, that's the very reason they put rubbers on the ends of pencils.

FLEABAG (*to* BOO). To fuck hamsters?

BOO. No, because people make mistakes.

FLEABAG. But now Boo's gone it's a death café so no one comes in. Hilary just sits in her hutch like a lump. Staring at me. I don't know what to do with her.

–

Six o'clock. Two yoga-body girls come into the café and order risotto off the menu. I pop to Tesco. Microwave their economy meal. The girls were talking about never wanting to give birth, because of what it'll do to their sex lives.

Still haven't heard from my sister.

I put an empty crisp packet in the microwave and watch it shrivel.

Play with my phone for a bit.

–

BOO (*recorded voicemail*). Hi this is Boo. I can't come to the phone at the moment but leave a messiagio and I'll get back to you.

FLEABAG. Someone should probably disconnect that.

–

I start texting Tube Rodent. I apologise and apologise and send him a picture of my tits. He ends up sending me one back. I *think* it's of his cock.

–

My boyfriend before Harry used to make me send him pictures of my vagina wherever I was. Ten or eleven times a day. I'd have to go and lunge in a disabled toilet and take an attractive picture of my vagina. Which is not easy, on the whole. Specially as he always wanted a worm's-eye view. It often looked like someone had dropped a little bap, on its side, on the floor of a hairdresser's. And taken a photo of it.

One temping morning, he asked me to take photos of my favourite bits of my body.

I went to the disabled loo.

Mimes unbuttoning her top. Bored. Takes pictures of her breasts. Stands up. Mimes hitching up her skirt, pulling aside her knickers, takes pictures of her vagina. Bored.

Mimes buttoning up. Flicks through the photos. Bored. Chooses one. Send.

Puts phone away.

Beep beep.

Takes phone out.

EX-BOYFRIEND. Oh that is so hot. Send another one, you beautiful bitch.

Mimes unbuttoning her top. Bored. Takes pictures of her breasts. Stands up. Mimes hitching up her skirt, pulling aside her knickers, takes pictures of her vagina. Bored.

*Mimes buttoning up. Flicks through the photos. Bored.
Chooses one. Send.*

Puts phone away.

Beep beep.

Takes phone out.

Now say something so dirty you shock yourself. Send me
another picture. Oh God, I'm wanking.

FLEABAG. It exhausted me, but you've got to do it. Can't have
them looking elsewhere.

The boss banged on the disabled-loo door. It was my fourth
visit that morning.

BOSS. Is everything alright in there?

FLEABAG. He's Australian.

(*To* BOSS.) Yeah – I've – I've just – got cystitis.

BOSS. Oh you poor chickadee! My wife gets that all the time!
Cranberry juice is what you need. Buckets of it. Shall I get
you some from the canteen?

Hon?

Hello?

Are you crying?

–

FLEABAG. I'm going to stop waxing. I met a man who said –
I say 'said' it was more of a yell – how much he loved a 'full
bush' and how 'rare they are these days'. Although it was
inappropriate at the time – family friend at Mum's funeral –
it filled me up with something. Hope? Relief? I don't know.
Can't bring myself to grow one.

–

I call Tube Rodent. He comes to the café with a bottle of wine. We drink it.

He whispers to me

TUBE RODENT. I have an enormous penis.

FLEABAG. I say: really? He says

TUBE RODENT. Yeah.

FLEABAG. I say: well that's lucky, because I have an enormous vagina. He says

TUBE RODENT (*confused*). Awesome.

FLEABAG. We fuck behind the counter. He's very bony. All corners. It's like having sex with a protractor. He doesn't come. He says I'm being too intense, whatever that means.

We turned the lights off and it's quite dark now. He's pulling on his trousers, looking for his phone to see if his friends are going out later. He's wearing this pink-and-purpley paisley scarf. He looks like a lady.

He hops over to the window and leans on the sill. He turns his phone on and he screams. Really high-pitched. The light from the phone made Hilary's eyes flash red in the darkness. She must have wandered over to the window while we were having sex.

For a second I laugh at his reaction, but she moves, and he screams again. She tries to run towards me, but she panics and sort of slips off the side. She lands on her stomach and struggles a bit, but Tube Rodent sees red and kicks her.

She flies against the wall with a thud.

He stares at the furry pile on the floor.

But she twitches. It makes him jump. He kicks her again. She goes flying across the floor.

I can't move. I think about Boo. I think about them playing together.

Tube Rodent's panicking. Mumbling something about a rat phobia.

I tell him he can go, and he disappears.

Hilary is on her front, but her back is to me. She looks like a... furry bullet.

She's still alive, but...

I put her back in her hutch and we just sit for a bit.

–

I text arsehole guy. He texts back saying he has a girlfriend and was really drunk the other night, but would love to hang out in a non-sex way. Sorry if he led me on.

I send my ex a picture of my vagina.

I send Harry a picture of my vagina.

I text Lily.

Still nothing from my sister.

Hilary's not moving.

BOO (*recorded voicemail*). Hi this is Boo. I can't come to the phone at the moment but leave a messiagio and I'll get back to you.

FLEABAG. Hilary starts making a horrible, chattering noise. I take her out of her hutch again. I put her on my lap. I stroke her, but she doesn't stop. I put her back.

–

I go to The Rabbit and Winslow pub. I smoke outside. Three people are laughing by the door. I can just make out the braces and the white hair through the crowd.

I can hear him.

Someone's let him on stage with his ukulele. He's singing a song. People are laughing and clapping.

I listen to it from outside. It's about a train ride he once took through Ireland, where a man told stories to everyone about love and home and romance and adventure and surprises and beautiful women and beautiful men and mothers and daughters and fathers and sons and monsters and fairies and parties and wishes...

All the usual crap.

The whole scene is something out of a revolting romcom, but he's nailing it.

He goes to the bar afterwards. Everyone buys him drinks. The man doesn't need to work.

I realise I've forgotten to give Hilary her Earl Grey.

–

Ten thirty at night. I hammer and hammer and ring the bell. I can see his silhouette at the top of the stairs but he doesn't open the door.

–

Back at the flat. Harry has obviously been round. The TV has gone and it smells like he did a shit. He never used to shit in the flat. He was really weird about it. Used to go to the pub over the road.

–

Sit on my stripy sofa. Open my laptop.

Anal

Gang bang

Mature

Big cocks

Small tits

Hentai

Asian

Teen

Milf

Big butt

Gay

Lesbian

Facial

Fetish

Young and old

Swallow

Rough

Voyeur

Public

Suddenly the sun's creeping in and I'm raw.

Lease is up today. Still nothing from my sister. I leave the flat.

–

BOO (*recorded voicemail*). Hi this is Boo…

–

FLEABAG. I put the closing sign up outside the café.

Three minutes past eleven. He's not here yet. I watch the door.

Ten past.

The door flies open.

JOE. Alright, baba ghanoush! Forgive me – I'm a little late, but do I have a morning story for you today or what! Listen to this –

FLEABAG. I tell him to shut up and close the door. He looks confused. But he does it.

(*To* JOE.) Why do you come here, Joe?

JOE. What?

FLEABAG. I close the blind and lock the door.

(*To* JOE.) Why do you come here, Joe?

JOE. Tea, love. And to see my ladies.

FLEABAG. Hilary's still not moving.

(*To* JOE.) It's okay, Joe. I understand. There's nothing wrong with you.

I take off my top. Unhook my bra. Place them gently on the counter.

He stares at me. I step forward. Showing him my young tits.

He shuffles a bit. His breathing changes. He's trembling.

He moves his hand up.

–

Nine o'clock that morning. My sister's door.

Martin's looking down at me.

MARTIN. Hello, you.

FLEABAG. Is Claire here?

MARTIN. Aye.

FLEABAG. I try to get past him into the house. He doesn't let me.

Claire comes to the door. She's crimped her fringe. I deliver a beautifully constructed joke about it. She snaps at me. Says I have to stop talking to people like I'm doing a stand-up routine. That some things just aren't fucking funny.

I laugh. And then I don't laugh. My throat goes dry. No one says anything for a bit.

(*To* SISTER.) You didn't transfer the money…

SISTER. No.

FLEABAG. You're not going to Finland.

SISTER. No.

FLEABAG. Why is he still here?

SISTER. He didn't touch you.

FLEABAG. He tried.

SISTER. He said it was more like the other way round.

FLEABAG. That's not true.

SISTER. How can I believe you?

FLEABAG. What? Because I'm your –

SISTER. After what you did to Boo.

FLEABAG (*to audience*). That wasn't my fault. He wanted me… he… wanted me so…

–

It's eleven fifteen now.

Joe is shaking.

I'm standing. Topless. Just the right angle.

His hand keeps rising, until it rests on his eyes.

JOE. Put your clothes back on, darling.

FLEABAG. What?

JOE. Put your clothes back on.

FLEABAG. Come on, Joe. I'm not going to judge you.

JOE. I come here for my tea, darling. And to see you. That was a sad thing that happened to your friend.

FLEABAG. You're weak.

JOE. That may be true, but… I'm going to go now.

FLEABAG. Stay. Come on. Please. Joe. I'm twenty-six years old, Joe.

He stops. He brings his hand down from his eyes. He finally looks at me.

JOE. Go home, darling. I'm sorry. This ain't my bag.

FLEABAG. I grab his arm as he walks past. He's thin but baggy. His skin pinches in my grasp. It's disgusting.

The door closes behind him.

–

I sit on Joe's chair for a bit. There's something not right about that man.

Hilary's teeth are going again. Crashing against each other. The noise is unbearable. Relentless chattering. They do that when they're distressed or angry or – I can't listen to it. I take her out of her hutch. I hold her little body to my naked chest. I can feel her claws. She can hardly move. Her bones feel bent and her breathing is shallow. But her teeth are going like – she won't – I stroke her body. I look into her face through her ginger, punky bit. I imagine sticking my finger in to make her eyes pop out. I imagine it. I imagine doing that – I can't imagine doing anything else and as my hand moves down her body – I – I –

When I first gave her to Boo she was so tiny. I put her in a little gift box from a crappy card shop. She just sat there on a bit of cotton wool. Looking up through her tiny punky bit. She was ridiculous. A little overexcited fuzzball. She'd just sit in your hand like – (*Makes a mini-explosion sound.*)

Boo's face. Boo's face when she opened the box – a huge grin spread across her whole body.

BOO. What is this!? Is this a guine– Did you get me a – What – What is this!?

FLEABAG. I don't know. Something to love?

I'm crying. My fingers are gripping her. I can't – I imagine my – I can't – I can feel how scared she is. How much pain she's in – My fingers are – I can't – I hold her to me tightly and – I hold her to me tighter… I hold her to me tighter, until I feel her bones crack against me and her chattering stop.

Everything is quiet and she is safe.

–

MALE VOICE. Okay. Please leave.

FLEABAG. What!? But I – you don't understand. I need –

MALE VOICE. Please just leave.

FLEABAG *starts to leave. She turns back.*

FLEABAG. Perv.

MALE VOICE. Slut.

FLEABAG. Wow.

MALE VOICE. Please leave.

FLEABAG. You please leave.

MALE VOICE. It's my office.

FLEABAG. Yeah?

MALE VOICE. Okay.

Sound effect of feet walking away and a door opening.

FLEABAG. Wait.

Footsteps stop.

What made you laugh?

MALE VOICE. What?

FLEABAG. On my CV. You said it was funny.

MALE VOICE. Um. You wrote that you run a café for guinea pigs…?

FLEABAG. Right. That's not strictly true but, okay. That made you laugh?

MALE VOICE. Yes. I suppose. Never thought guinea pigs needed –

FLEABAG. It was a guinea-pig-themed café.

MALE VOICE. Oh right.

FLEABAG. Yeah.

MALE VOICE. That makes sense.

FLEABAG. Yeah.

What if I wrote that I fucked that café into liquidation, that I fucked up my family, I fucked my friend by fucking her boyfriend, that I don't feel alive unless I'm being fucked and I don't feel in control unless I'm fucking, because fucking makes the world tighten around me, that I've been watching people fuck for as long as I've been able to search for it, that I know that my body as it is now is really the only thing I have and when that gets old and unfuckable I might as well just kill it, that sometimes I wish I never knew fucking existed because somehow there isn't anything worse than someone who doesn't want to fuck me.

That I fuck everything. But *this* time, I genuinely wasn't trying to – I wasn't – I was –

Either everyone feels like this a little bit and they're just not talking about it, or I'm completely fucking alone. Which isn't fucking funny.

MALE VOICE. That really wasn't appropriate.

FLEABAG. Yeah. Okay. Sorry.

She goes to leave.

MALE VOICE. Look. Three months ago I touched a colleague's breast at a party. Not for the first time. It's ruined the reputation of the business I've been building my whole life and has completely alienated me from my family.

FLEABAG. Why did you do it?

MALE VOICE. I... It was a terrible... mistake.

FLEABAG. People make mistakes.

MALE VOICE. Yes they do.

FLEABAG. That's why they put rubbers on the ends of pencils.

MALE VOICE (*little laugh*). Is that a joke?

FLEABAG. I don't know.

MALE VOICE. Shall we… start this interview again?

FLEABAG. Okay.

MALE VOICE. Thanks for coming in. Really appreciate you sending in your CV.

FLEABAG. No problem.

MALE VOICE. It was funny.

She laughs.

FLEABAG. Fuck you.

End.

www.nickhernbooks.co.uk

facebook.com/nickhernbooks

twitter.com/nickhernbooks